BASKETS
INDOORS
OUTDOORS
PRACTICAL
DECORATIVE

TEXT BY PIEN LEMSTRA
ARRANGEMENTS BY FERNANDE HORA SICCAMA
PHOTOGRAPHS BY HANS VAN OMMEREN

HARRY N. ABRAMS, INC., PUBLISHERS

Translated from the Dutch by Mieke Wilson-van Leeuwe

Library of Congress Cataloging-in-Publication Data

Lemstra, Pien.
    Baskets / text by Pien Lemstra ; flower arrangements by Fernande
Hora Siccama ; photographs by Hans van Ommeren.
      p.   cm.
    Includes index.
    ISBN 0–8109–3136–2
    1. Basket making.   2. Basketwork.   I. Title.
TT879.B3L45   1995
746.41'2— dc20   94-20425

❧ Contents ❧

❧ *Introduction* ❧

The words "nature" and "basket" have a close relationship. The basket, being made of natural materials, is extremely useful for holding natural produce. Living as we do in an age dominated by speed, artificial products, and technology, and when the atmosphere around us is polluted by exhaust gases and acid rain, it becomes more important to surround ourselves with "real" things. Fortunately, we are taking more care of our environment and beginning to move away from using artificial materials. These days, we are less enthusiastic about cool, white decor in our homes and are turning more to color, and to foliage and flowers, beautifully displayed in natural containers.

It is clear that baskets have played a part in our early history. In ancient Egypt, for example, making baskets and mats was a real art, and in addition to all the silver and gold artifacts in Tutankhamun's tomb, there were also beautiful baskets. From the Bible, we are all familiar with the story of Moses's

basket in the bulrushes. A very old stratagem used in Egypt in Moses's time was for Egyptian warriors to hide themselves in baskets to get themselves transported into a besieged town. Could it be that these "Egyptian baskets" were the inspiration for the Greek Trojan Horse?

Baskets have been made and used in North America for thousands of years. Today, early Native American baskets are prized by museums and private collectors.

In this book we make a special journey through the world of baskets. We will visit many countries, because each society has its own baskets, made for local use and created with local materials. Some baskets are crudely made, others skillfully; some are uneven and rough, some are of a finer quality. They are made of branches of wood, rush, rattan, broom, olive wood, and willow twigs.

In France we found traditional wooden

Left: Baskets are ideal natural containers for gathering and displaying flowers and foliage.

grape-harvesting baskets and baskets made of braided vine branches. We admired the beautifully crafted baskets made in the Philippines, where people still make and paint baskets in the traditional way. In their cheerful colors, these modern baskets make an exotic contrast with the coarse, handcrafted willow baskets that you might find in the Netherlands.

We admired Italian wire baskets, English harvesting baskets, American baskets made of tree bark, and Dutch potato baskets with special holes at the bottom to allow the soil to fall through. We compared coarse dark baskets from Portugal with exotic bamboo and rattan baskets from the Far East. Each one exudes its own atmosphere, its own culture.

We found that many baskets are essential in our daily life, a fact that surprised us. We rediscovered the household basket for dust cloths and rags, the dog basket, and the shopping basket. We were seized by "basketmania" and discovered that more people are suffering from this disease; people who like anything that has been made of natural materials, people who like baskets, who appreciate the toughness of the material, the variety of techniques involved in making them, their warmth and decorative value. These people fill their houses with baskets and with the colors and scents of nature. They want to surround themselves with these natural products as a bastion against today's wasteful society.

We filled the baskets that we found on our journey with an abundance of color and fragrance, and the splendid flower arrangements show off the form and structure of the baskets to full advantage. On the following pages we demonstrate both the functional and decorative value of the baskets, and offer advice and suggestions on how to use the baskets, arrange flowers, and brighten up your home and garden with basketry.

All this material has been compiled by Fernande Hora Siccama and Hans van Ommeren. Their love of nature and baskets inspired them to produce both the wonderful flower arrangements and the superb artistic photographs of them. The result of this cooperation is a book in which you will find a festival of foliage, flowers, and beautiful baskets – a profusion of colors that will inspire you every time you look at it. I recorded their progress with great admiration as I followed them in their work.

I hope you will enjoy all these baskets and become infected with our "basketmania."

Pien Lemstra

Handcrafted baskets made from willow rods

Basket making is a traditional craft that dates back many centuries, and many beautiful and practical examples are found worldwide. In the Netherlands, for example, the craft is handed down from one generation to another, and the weavers featured in the photographs on the following pages are continuing a production process that is exactly the same as the one employed by their fathers and grandfathers. They in turn have handed down their craft to the next generations, and it is encouraging to know that their sons and grandsons are acquiring the same skills. They make a variety of beautiful, strong baskets intended for everyday use, such as the square, flat ones in which bakers display their bread. They make potato baskets and baskets for potato peelings, laundry baskets, and shopping baskets.

Dutch basket makers have always played an important role in their society because their

products were ideal for storing and transporting a wide variety of everyday essentials. Bakers loaded baskets onto their carts and bicycles, eggs and dairy products were packed into them, and they were ideal for storing vegetables, such as potatoes, or fresh foods, including fish. Baskets were used to transport animals – chickens, eels, cats, pigeons, and ducks all had baskets designed to carry them – and there was even a beehive basket. Baskets had their place in the home as well, whether as a cradle, a shopping basket, a wastepaper basket, or a place for storage. In industry, baskets were used for coal, bulbs, and shrubs. Dutch basket makers still make "growing" baskets, which have an unfinished appearance, with their long, upward-pointing stakes secured at the top with wicker. In the olden days, they were used to transport plants and shrubs. The plants, with their rootballs attached,

Left: *Each basket tells a story. Made from natural materials and fashioned by industrious hands, they have earned their own place in society.*

Left: *Traditionally, the weaver works sitting on the floor on boards. The willow he is using has been harvested alongside streams and riverbeds nearby.*

Left: *These traditional Dutch baskets come in all shapes, sizes, styles, and colors, and are designed for a wide variety of uses, both indoors and outdoors.*

Right: *Dutch basket makers continue a long tradition and pass on the art of making their solid, handcrafted baskets to the next generation.*

were put into the woven "growing" baskets and the foliage was tied to the long stakes. (You can see examples of these baskets on page 17.) Today they are back in demand. As we found, they make wonderful containers for ivies, sweet peas, and nasturtiums, which can climb naturally up the stakes to make a beautiful and fragrant display indoors, on a balcony, or in the garden. Clematis or small varieties of climbing roses are just as effective when grown in this way, and if you choose to grow non-hardy plants, you can bring them indoors, with their basket, for the winter.

After World War II, baskets were replaced by less labor-intensive packing materials. The wicker basket slowly disappeared from daily life until the 1970s, when people began to turn away from plastic and other cold, artificial materials and rediscovered the aesthetic value of natural, handcrafted products. Today, baskets are fashionable once again. They embody our desire for practical but natural products in our homes and gardens, and in almost every household you will find baskets made from a variety of materials in everyday use. Never before has the supply and choice of baskets been so extensive or the demand so great. Hand-crafted goods generally are enjoying a revival in popularity, and this includes baskets made by traditional basket makers.

Using willow for basket making

Almost all European handcrafted baskets are made of willow. Most are made from *Salix triandra* (almond-leaved willow), but other varieties used include *Salix viminalis* (common osier), and *Salix alba* 'Vitellina' (golden willow). Although willow is not an aquatic plant, willow beds are found near freshwater rivers. Willow is propagated by planting cuttings at a depth of about 8" (20 cm). These soon root and grow, and if the ground is well-managed, willow trees will continue to produce rods for 20 to 30 years. In the fall and winter, the willow is cut as short as possible – a process known as "pollarding," which encourages the dense growth of young shoots.

Traditionally, willow was cut by hand with a bill hook, but today it is carried out mechanically with a special harvesting machine. The willow rods are sorted by length and quality, and sold in bundles, or bolts, to be used as binding or braiding wicker. In the Netherlands, most of the willow is exported to Germany, Belgium, and France, where binding willow is used for bunching and tying vine branches. Only one hectare (100 acres) of the entire willow yield is used for basket making in the Netherlands itself.

We are still finding new ways of using willow as a decorative material. One idea is to buy bundles of willow and display them as a

Above: Here, sheaves of rush tied with pink ribbon form a natural curtain on either side of a window. The dark brown wicker basket filled with pink Hydrangea macrophylla echoes the colors of the rush curtain and its ribbon ties.

Above: *The fresh green of the shooting willow matches the green of the stylish glass bowl. It stands on the sill of an arched window, just above a pair of apple-green candles displayed in Empire pewter candlesticks.*

feature in their own right. They look very effective on either side of a door, in shop window displays, or next to large mirrors. You can transform them into special bouquets by fastening colorful ribbons around the upright stakes. To create the arrangement shown in the photograph on the left, we put a bundle of willow in a bucket of water and concealed the bucket in a willow apple basket with a paper ribbon around it. After a few weeks, the willow started to shoot, and the room was adorned with a small sheaf of growing willow.

Light and dark baskets

The willow used for making baskets differs greatly in color, from very dark brown to almost white. The darker the color, the older the wicker: young, fresh willow is very light. However, a difference in color can also have a lot to do with whether the bark is stripped off the willow. Dark baskets are made of unstripped willow, whereas white ones are made of stripped willow, which can itself vary in color. Very light-colored willow is stripped with a tool called a willow-stripping brake, or in a machine with a rotating drum. Then it is dried and bleached in the sun.

Another method of treating willow is known as barking, or peeling the bark. In this case, the rods are boiled until the bark disintegrates and falls away. Boiling has the

Right: Here, hydrangeas have been planted in round baskets. Birch branches formed into hoops are pushed into the soil around the baskets and form a support for ivy to climb up. A little bird with a pale pink breast the same color as the hydrangeas sits on top of the hoop. Spray the baskets regularly with water, as hydrangeas also absorb some moisture through their petals, and after a while the birch branches will begin to shoot and form a green nest for the bird. The flowering currant trees growing in the background add a magical white haze to the scene.

effect of staining the wood, because the tannic acids in the bark penetrate the rods and give them a pleasing bronze-brown color. This is known as buff-willow.

How you select which baskets to buy and use is largely a matter of taste. The baskets used every day by bakers, on bicycles, for pets, or for going shopping are mostly made from boiled buff-willow. Whether you prefer light, stripped wicker, light brown, smooth buff-willow, or dark, unstripped wicker, there is no shortage of examples to choose from to suit every home and application.

Left: *Bundles of willow. The reddish-brown bundle in the middle is buff-willow. There are various methods of treating willow to achieve the range of colors seen in the baskets in use today.*

Right: *A green duck's nest sits happily between some "growing" baskets. You can fill these baskets with ivy, clematis, nasturtiums, and other climbers and train the plants to climb the stakes.*

Right: A seventeenth-century Dutch mill. Thatching is another example of a specialized handicraft, and thatching windmills is an exceptional skill. In the Netherlands there are many octagonal-shaped thatched mills. Thatching these mills requires great skill and is complicated by the slope of the structure and the vibration of the working windmill. This complex work can only be done by "mill thatchers." Some mills have a decorative relief, which is usually found on the side visible from the road. In earlier times, thatchers used to include the year, some initials, or a pattern into the thatch by tapping it with a wooden tool at certain points where the thatch was less thick.

This mill has been completely renovated by its present owners. The part shown here is called the cap and dates from 1694. It has been thatched down to the stage, or platform.

Above: Two baskets, similar in size and shape to a stork's nest, stand on either side of the mill house door. They are supported on stakes in the shape of a tripod. Each basket is 39" (1 m) in diameter and can hold many plants. These baskets are filled with a profusion of ivy (Hedera) and impatiens. The blooms match the pink sweet peas (Lathyrus) in the charming heart-shaped arrangement hanging on the front door.

Left: This stork's nest, supported on a metal stand in a meadow, is perfectly reflected in the water. Do not expect any birds to nest here, however, as the basket is purely decorative and placed in this position for maximum visual impact. From the Renaissance onwards, people have used optical effects and perspective in landscape gardening to guide the eye of the beholder. You could say that this view is framed and conveys a suggestion of infinity.

Right: A shallow, dark brown wicker basket graces a conference table. The single stem of bougainvillea in the center is surrounded by smaller varieties of bougainvillea and ferns (Nephrolepis exaltata). Pale pink sweet peas are tucked in to fill the gaps.

Above: The same stork's nest situated indoors creates a completely different effect. The flowers in this handcrafted basket add warmth to the simply furnished, modern, oriental embassy interior. Pink begonias compete gracefully with trailing ivies, impatiens, and pale pink Spiraea. A basket of this size can hold a wide variety of plants, and the mass of flowers contrasts beautifully with the brown texture of the basket.

Exotic baskets made of rattan and bamboo

Most of the baskets we buy today have been imported from the Far East. The reasons for this are not purely economic; although it is true that baskets from the Far East are very cheap, they also reveal a high level of craftsmanship and their design is often unusual and exotic. The baskets are made mostly of rattan and bamboo, extremely strong materials that grow in abundance in that part of the world.

One country that exports baskets is the Philippines, where basketry is a very old and traditional craft; in fact, making baskets could be said to be part of the country's history. Drawings, dating from the earliest times, depict baskets belonging to street vendors, fishermen, travelers, and traders, and these traditions are still seen in modern baskets. Until the early 1970s, the native islanders made baskets mainly for their own use,

but then the basket trade began to enjoy a worldwide revival as more and more people started to collect beautiful, as well as functional, artifacts including baskets. In the Philippines, materials were plentiful and there was no shortage of craftsmen, so the country found it easy to meet the large demand for its products. Each island and region has its own traditional design and these individual ways of making baskets, the creative designs and use of different materials, have become famous all over the world.

As well as modern designs, craftsmen still make traditional baskets for everyday use. Originally, the baskets changed color over a period of time until they became a velvety dark brown as a result of prolonged exposure to smoke and strong sunlight. Nowadays, this color is reproduced artificially to achieve the same effect.

Left: In the Philippines, basketry is an integral part of culture and tradition, just as it is in the Netherlands. Today, baskets made in the Far East are available all over the world.

Left: These modern baskets are as charming as the traditional ones. The square basket with a lid is filled with cooked rice for the midday meal and taken to the fields – a basket lunchbox.

Making rattan baskets

To make rattan baskets, the bark is split into extremely long strips, which are then woven into variously shaped baskets. Sometimes the strips are twisted during the weaving, which creates a distinctive pattern. As the baskets are used, dirt and grease form a patina on the baskets, accentuating the pattern even more. The smooth top parts acquire the dark brown color more quickly than the coarser bottom parts, and this difference in color creates a pattern. These days the difference in color is carefully imitated to make the baskets look authentically old. Most of these baskets were used for storing vegetables and other food. Usually they had a lid and were fixed to a wooden stand with rattan strips. As the baskets were often kept underneath the house, the wooden stand formed a firm base for the basket, which was quite often filled to the brim. Most baskets are oddly shaped, as they were made in a hurry and packed tight, but it is these little imperfections that give them their charm and authenticity.

Left: These large, plate-shaped baskets are made from rattan strips. The base has a different pattern from the sides, and in time the colors change, making the patterns quite distinctive.

Above: This open-weave rattan container filled with pears was originally a draining basket. It would have been suspended above the fire to drain and dry washed wooden spoons.

Left: *This handled basket, filled with a dried pink hydrangea, is a perfect match for the old stones of the street and wall behind it. It is made in the style of a vegetable storage basket, in which a farmer would have regularly carried his fresh produce to market.*

Right: *These days, baskets are manufactured mainly for export. Western influences are clearly visible in the shapes and colors, as the baskets are subject to modern commercial and fashion requirements. They are mostly made of rattan, bamboo, or rush, and are often painted, either in soft pastel shades, bright hues, or old, natural colors. They may even be painted with European-style designs. This blue-edged, white potato basket is decorated with red apples. It is filled with red Dutch apples and looks traditionally Dutch, but in fact it was made in the Philippines.*

Left: Do not be deceived by the Delft-blue pattern on this cachepot made of rattan bark strips; it comes from the Philippines. The edges are made of wood and joined to the basket with rattan strips. White prairie gentian (Eustoma grandiflora) and gray lavender are planted in the pot, which is flanked by two antique Chinese porcelain jars.

Right: Orange zinnias and nasturtiums in front of an old stable. The woven rattan basket on a wooden stand is painted in shades of brown.

Left: Here are two more cachepots planted with lavender. The solid, dark brown troughs are made from strong bamboo stakes, held together at the edges with rattan strips. The troughs are especially suitable for outdoors and are available in several colors. They have been painted by rubbing paint into the wood with a cloth to produce a soft hint of color.

Above: *This solid onion basket is a modern product from the Philippines. It is made of rattan with wooden edges, then painted red – a* *perfect match for the onions and onion bag. The handles are shaped like butterflies, which gives the whole thing an oriental feel. Compare* *this with the plain Dutch harvesting basket behind it; a good example of East meeting West outside the kitchen door.*

The ageless appeal of natural rattan

Basketry is one of the oldest known crafts. In the seventeenth century, the idea of using glossy cane, or rattan, for the backs and seats of chairs was introduced into Europe from China and became very popular. It was brought to England from France at this time to replace the heavy and rather gloomy furnishings of the Tudor period. Interior decorators became very interested in rattan in the 1950s when it was highly popular, and today it is back in fashion once more.

The extensive labor involved in the production of rattan is undertaken mainly in the Far East, in countries such as the Philippines and Indonesia. Baskets made of natural rattan come in all shapes and sizes. They are designed for everyday use, are beautiful in color and structure, and are of a high quality. Often, rattan products are more expensive than, say, willow ones, because rattan is more expensive and needs extensive preparation before it is ready to use. However, as it is more durable than other materials, it is well worth the extra cost, particularly if you are buying items of furniture.

Right: Rattan is very strong. Once lacquered, baskets can safely be left outside, as they are resistant to the effects of wind and rain. Their color fades, but that, too, has a charm of its own. Treated rattan baskets and good-quality furniture can last for up to 30 years.

Above: Dried hydrangeas are stored in an oriental basket made of stripped bamboo with wrought-iron handles and edges.

Right: Lacquered baskets with strong handles. The walking sticks and baskets are ideal partners.

The Philippine baskets on the right have been lacquered. In a way, the baskets with the walking sticks are a joint venture. The sticks are made of bamboo and imported into Europe, where the baskets are then worked around them. You can use the walking sticks out in the garden, in the woods, or in the fields, and fill the baskets with the fruits of nature as you walk along. The strong bamboo walking stick will withstand the rain and support you through the mud, and when you are tired you can lean on it.

The baskets are often placed on woven, willow fences that are both functional and decorative. The beauty of a fence like this is that outdoors the willow will eventually begin to shoot again and make a "living" fence. Sometimes these leafy fences are used as a sound barrier along highways, where they provide a welcome contrast to the black, asphalt roads and the metallic shine of the cars. For the people living behind these natural sound barriers, they must make a welcome sight, as well as improving the general environment.

These fences also have a place in the home, where they can be used as a screen, a room divider, or to conceal an unattractive wall. And their application does not stop there; in shops, they make an unusual and attractive wall for displaying merchandise.

Outdoor baskets — part of the landscape

You can use baskets anywhere, indoors or outdoors. Being made of natural material, they seem to belong outside, where they become part of the landscape, a fragment of nature. If you do not have a yard, but have to content yourself with a balcony or terrace, then baskets seem to fit particularly well into the patio garden. They look just as much at home in city surroundings. A wicker basket filled with flowering plants on the beautiful old steps of a tall stately house is a sign that nature has not been forgotten.

If baskets are left standing on a damp surface for any length of time, the base will soon start to rot and disintegrate, but this does not really matter. If the plant has become rooted in the basket, some of the roots will find their way through the base and establish themselves in the ground. Many baskets intended for outdoor use, such as

harvesting baskets, Sussex baskets, or trugs, and grape baskets, have bases reinforced with a wooden rim. Others have little legs to lift the basket above the surface and protect the woven base. However, if a basket is rotten and you can no longer use it outside, try the following idea. Place the basket in a pond around a waterlily. The basket will float and you will have created a rather unusual aquatic bouquet.

Baskets are ideal for displaying nonhardy plants outdoors. Obviously, you will have to bring the plants inside as soon as the colder weather sets in, and this is when you will appreciate the advantages of using baskets as containers. They are much lighter than pots and therefore easier to move, and they will neither freeze nor break. They are just as suitable for hardy plants. Their naturally dark color perfectly

Left: A large wicker basket filled with hydrangeas, ivy, and Santolina chamaecyparissus. The cool colors are echoed in the ornamental gray stone shelf support by the front door.

Left: Do not feel you have to throw away a basket if its base has rotted away. Float it on a pond around a waterlily, and it makes an unusual yet natural frame for the blooms.

Left: *A strawberry plant in a wicker "bird's nest." The amusing effect suggests that strawberries have been laid in the nest instead of eggs. Dark green* Hosta *leaves and olive-green moss form an excellent background for the red of the strawberries, and the moss also acts as a soft bed for the fruits during the growing season.*

Above: *This basket of strawberries has been made to a more traditional design. It is supported on a screen woven from buff-willow. Behind the screen are large bundles of the willow from which the screen was made.*

Above: *Six tiny baskets filled with apples, cooking pears, and blackberries create a miniature fall display on a pretty, green garden table. Fall colors also feature in the basket display above the bench.*

complements the green foliage of the plants inside them. While the baskets are standing outside, they gradually weather and fade, and, if anything, this makes them even more beautiful than before.

Baskets in the garden

Coarse, solid baskets are especially suitable for outdoor use. They are reasonably resistant to damp and rainy weather, and as they age and are exposed to the elements they become even more attractive. They are ideal for non-hardy plants and shrubs that you wish to move inside for the winter. Being light, baskets are easy to lift and carry about. If you leave them outside all winter, exposed to rain and frost, the base will inevitably rot. As we have seen, this does not mean you have to discard them. As well as floating them on water around pond plants, you can put them around thin-stemmed flowering plants with heavy flowerheads, such as delphiniums and peonies. The basket not only functions as a natural support, it also looks attractive. The flower spikes of the delphiniums and the rounded peony blooms will actually look as though they are growing in the basket.

Left: Displayed on this little terrace is a whole collection of beautiful examples of box topiary growing in dark, unstripped willow baskets. The box variety is Buxus sempervirens, an evergreen with small green leaves.

Box plants in baskets

Box *(Buxus)* is a slow-growing evergreen shrub that will grow in a basket as long as it has plenty of space. Give it a regular feed of bonemeal in spring, just before the growing season. During mild winters, box can remain outside, but as the plants are rather tender, take care that the soil around them does not freeze. If you cannot bring them inside, cover them with straw, jute, or plastic. If you do bring them indoors, keep them in a light, cool place, such as a hall, garage, conservatory, or greenhouse.

Box is ideal for trimming and training into ornamental shapes. The topiary examples in the photograph opposite are quite large and therefore quite old – ten to twelve years at least. The ball with the proud chicken on top is much older. They are pruned just once a year, preferably in midsummer. Pruning is a special art; the ball with the chicken on top is a masterpiece and could only have been created by someone with many years experience. The chicken shape itself is the result of years of expert pruning. Do not be afraid of making mistakes if you want to try your hand at topiary. It is great fun experimenting, and you can always start with a simple shape, such as a ball or a pyramid. In Roman times, special slaves were employed for pruning box.

Haddonstone containers

Haddonstone vases, baskets, and garden ornaments are famous throughout Europe. Haddonstone is specially designed to imitate limestone. It looks exactly like hewn limestone, but is easy to manufacture and less expensive than the real thing. It is resistant to every kind of weather and often used in the restoration of old buildings and sculptures. When it is new, Haddonstone is very clean and light gray in color, but after it has been outside for a while it really comes "alive." The stone is porous and as it weathers, moss starts to grow on it, giving it an aged, even antique appearance. You can speed up the process of growing moss on the stone by rubbing the outside surfaces with yogurt.

The Haddonstone collection is famous for its detailed reproductions of classical designs by great Italian sculptors, such as Michelangelo. Garden ornaments, vases, and urns are often copies of originals found in English country houses and castles. The most well-known pieces are the pineapple, the fruit

Right: Bunches of ivy, eucalyptus, and dark blue berries have been arranged in Haddonstone baskets. One of the baskets is on a Haddonstone bench with an attractive decorative edge.

baskets, and the lion. The basket-weave container featured on pages 40-41 is a copy of an old English design, and it is resting on a Haddonstone bench with legs in the shape of a lion's paws, although these are not visible on the photograph. Behind the bench is a garden mirror that lends the scene a mysterious air. Garden mirrors are large, shiny glass balls, usually placed in the middle of a flowerbed so that colorful masses of flowers are reflected in the shining glass. In the nineteenth century, ladies taking tea looked surreptitiously into the mirror to see exactly what was happening behind them, so that the mirrors became a sort of spy glass. There are also suggestions that shiny glass balls drive away witches, since witches are not allowed to look into a mirror (hence the common name of witches' balls).

Left: *These square, low baskets, some decoratively edged with flower shapes, are particularly suited to walled gardens. Here, they are grouped on the ground and filled with several varieties of thyme. The Haddonstone "fruit" basket and the pineapple on a pedestal are also distinctive and striking designs.*

Wire baskets — ancient and modern

In the countryside in France you often see old farmers' wives going to market with their wire egg baskets, rusted and twisted with age. These round wire containers are just the right shape for storing eggs and have little legs to protect the eggs from damage when the basket is placed on the ground. They are also used to collect the eggs, and there is no risk of them toppling over onto the straw, soil, or mud. You can still find these baskets in antique shops, at auctions, or bric-a-brac sales, and if you have a particular passion for baskets, there is nothing more exciting than browsing at leisure and unearthing more examples to add to your collection. It does not matter how rusty and twisted they are, they are all equally endearing. Once back home, you can store your eggs in a genuine egg basket and hang up your other "finds" to decorate the kitchen. Wire egg baskets are still made today, and

Left: Eggs were traditionally stored in wire baskets. You can still find original examples of these baskets, or buy modern ones to use in your kitchen.

you need not use them just for eggs. For example, the one in the shape of a chicken in the photograph below is filled with onions.

A very familiar basket is the plastic-coated wire hanging basket. You see them everywhere, decorating the outside of houses, sheds, garages, and pergolas, and filled with masses of geraniums, petunias and gray-leaved salvias. Hanging at the front door, they make visitors feel welcome, and in gardens or on terraces they form a focal point. You can create perfect, tiny hanging gardens in a basket. Round hanging baskets come in three sizes – small, medium, and large, and you hang them up by three chains linked to a ring. To use these baskets, you must first line them with sphagnum moss and then with a layer of plastic with holes pierced into it. Having lined them in this way, you can then fill them with potting mixture and plants. Hanging baskets are just

Left: A collection of wire baskets makes an unusual decorative feature. They look equally good empty or filled with fruit and vegetables.

as attractive indoors; try packing them with a mixture of trailing plants and hanging them in a bay window. You can use hanging baskets for storing vegetables and fruit, for keeping bulbs dry ready for planting the following year, and even for keeping odds and ends in the garage or attic. When you are looking for a suitable place to hang the basket, take its diameter into account and do not hang it too close to a wall.

Left: *This hanging basket beneath a light is filled with pale blue hydrangeas and* Ampelopsis. *The blue of the hydrangeas matches the blue-veined marble of the table, and the foliage echoes the green box growing under the table. Two Haddonstone dogs stand guard on either side of the front door.*

Above: *An aluminum wire basket on a green cast-iron bench with a wooden seat and back. The basket is filled with variegated ivy, ferns, and dwarf hydrangeas. Aluminum is very popular for baskets, as is zinc. Many of the new designs are made with a nod in the direction of the 1930s and 1940s, when all our buckets, tubs, and watering cans were made of zinc. Now they are made of galvanized metal.*

Left: *A basket of white roses and blue thistles. Line all wire baskets before adding any potting mixture or plants. You can leave the basket outside in the rain for a short time and then either hang it outdoors or bring it inside the house.*

Italian wire baskets

These Italian wire baskets are produced by Mondo. They are handmade according to traditional designs and are therefore rather expensive. The basket on the teak garden table has hooks around the sides. In Roman times, such baskets were filled with strawberries or figs, and little cups, supported on the hooks, contained cream, so that people could dip the fruit into the cream before eating it. Today, instead of fruit, the basket is lined with moss and planted with ferns and lilies-of-the-valley, and night lights burning in old clay flowerpots have replaced the cups of cream. The clay flowerpots are themselves enjoying a revival in popularity. Once they were used for cuttings from the garden until plastic pots took their place. Now these attractive, old, and often crooked clay pots – each one is unique – hold night lights or small candles, which absorb smoke from the air around.

The round basket with a scalloped rim, here filled with walnuts, is another example of an Italian Mondo wire basket. Next to it is a round bowl filled with pomanders, which have a spicy fragrance of cinnamon and cloves that goes well with walnuts and the fall. They help to create a medieval atmosphere, standing next to the "ancient" wire basket. To make a pomander, stick cloves into an apple, orange, or lemon, and roll the fruit through a

Above: These modern handmade wire baskets are copied from traditional designs. They can be used for a variety of decorative purposes indoors and out.

Right: Open-weave baskets are ideal for storing nuts and other fruits and vegetables that need air to circulate around them once they have been harvested.

mixture of equal amounts of cinnamon, nutmeg, and ground cloves. Allow the pomander to dry out a little before hanging it up. Alternatively, display the pomanders in a bowl. Placed on a bed of dried lavender flowers, they have a spicy fragrance that mixes with the sweet scent of the lavender.

Above: *The cake plate is yet another type of wire basket by Mondo. Here, instead of cakes, the flat wire plate on a stand displays little open-* *curled cabbages. Behind it, miniature red cabbages, also appetizingly displayed in a wire basket, are waiting to be used in a salad.*

Left: In this metal basket, a mixture of strawberries and blackberries are growing in moist sphagnum moss.

Left: This elegant container on a pedestal is another beautifully crafted Mondo basket. It is lined with moss and filled with an unusual display of blackberries, wild roses, and Artemisia leaves.

Above: *Here, four artichokes are arranged in front of some pale green hydrangeas that have been picked for drying. Both are displayed on a rectangular, galvanized metal tray, painted a grayish green color. The small, concrete dove is not just a decoration for the garden table; its gray body also complements the gray-green color of the leaves and the lilac-green of the dried hydrangeas and appetizing artichokes.*

Left: *Even more artichokes on a kitchen table. This genuine kitchen basket has a wooden frame with chicken wire wrapped around it, and is designed for carrying and storing vegetables. They look attractive in the basket and will keep fresh for a long time, as air circulates easily around them.*

Metal baskets

The flower basket on legs featured on the left is made by punching out a design from sheet metal and then welding curled legs onto the basket. Being rather large, these baskets are suitable for a variety of uses. This one was originally a jardinière, but here it is used as a container for vegetables and fruit. In this photograph, the basket catches the last rays of the sun at the end of the day. However, the fruit will not actually feel the sun's warmth, as it is made of wood. Painted in soft pastel shades, it looks deceptively real. The fruit is made in Indonesia, where beautiful wooden fruits are made in great quantities. You will not find apples and pears, though, as all the Indonesian fruits are tropical. In the background, a large Haddonstone flowerpot is filled with ivy and gray salvias.

Above: It would be lovely to warm yourself in front of an inviting brazier like this, especially during the cold winter months, and you can also roast apples or sweet chestnuts on it. The basket can be used on a terrace, in the garden, or even on a large balcony. To keep the fire going, you can burn charcoal or wood in the basket and even add leaves, dead wood, and other garbage from the garden if you have some to dispose of.

Left: *An iron wire basket decorated with leaded ribbon on a garden table covered with moss balls.*

Above: *Like the tray on page 52, this gray-green flower basket is made of galvanized wirework. A bowl filled with water and damp flower foam fits inside the basket to hold the arrangement of champagne-colored roses, blue thistle, and gray Kochia. Here, too, the gray-green color of a fall mist is captured in the combination of wild and cultivated garden flowers. Branches of Kochia, which dry easily, are tucked between the basket and the bowl to disguise the bowl.*

Baskets made of wood — pretty and practical

Up till now we have only discussed woven baskets, made of rods, twigs, and vine branches. However, wooden troughs and baskets from France, England, America, and Germany also have a place in this book.

The grape-harvesting basket from the wine-growing areas in France is one example. In most regions, the grape harvesters place the grapes they have picked in specially woven back baskets. In the Dordogne, the people make and use wooden grape-harvesting baskets. They are made from several different kinds of wood, are extremely strong and simple in shape. They taper towards the base so that the bunches of grapes automatically roll down. Grape troughs like the one on this page are widely exported for a variety of decorative purposes. They vary in size from 5" (13 cm) to 21½" (55 cm) across and have a handle made from a strong branch. This basket is nestling in a bed

Left: Wooden trugs are practical and pretty. Walking stick baskets are ideal in areas where tall flowers and foliage might obscure a low basket.

of *Alchemilla mollis*, or lady's mantle, with its beautiful, yellow lacelike flowers that bloom all summer. You can pick as many of the flowers as you wish, as it soon grows again. Lady's mantle is very useful in flower arrangements instead of foliage. When there is no more water left in the vase, the *Alchemilla* dries to a rusty yellow color and you can continue to use it as a dried flower.

English wooden harvesting baskets are well-known and used by gardeners to collect weeds or hold freshly picked flowers, but they are just as attractive when used to display, say, roses. You can also use them to store secateurs, garden twine, and gloves, so that you have everything you need to hand. The baskets have little legs so that they cannot sink into the ground, especially when it is wet. The baskets are made of chestnut and nailed together, and both the rim and the handle have the bark left on.

Left: Two "bird's nests" filled with red currants look very much at home in a wooden grape basket. These baskets have many decorative uses.

Walking stick baskets are a variation on the trug. They save you bending over and support you as you walk through the garden, or you can stick them in the ground where you are working – an excellent idea for forgetful gardeners who can always see where they have left their basket!

Expensive English trugs are very similar to the simple field baskets found in France and pictured at top right. There, every farmer makes a wooden basket for his wife so that she can collect a daily supply of produce from the vegetable garden. In small village markets, you can see the farmers' wives sitting on a chair under an umbrella or sometimes just standing by an old table selling carrots, beans, onions, and other items from their homemade wooden baskets.

The American basket on page 61 is made of bark fastened together with raffia. The base consists of thick slats placed parallel to one another with a small space in between. These bark baskets are very suitable for outside use, but look just as attractive indoors. You can use them as vases by putting a piece of wet flower foam in the basket and arranging flowers in it.

Top right: *This vegetable basket is typical of the ones that farmers' wives use in the French countryside.*

Bottom right: *This sturdy yet portable wooden "tool basket" is a variation of the homemade farmer's basket.*

Above: *This American basket contains a daring combination of various reds: roses, red as fire, are placed next to bold red poppies.*

Above: *An American basket made of short branches bound together with raffia, and filled with ferns and hydrangeas.*

Right: *This basket of ivies has been standing outside for several years and moss has started to grow on it. The color of the bark matches the mossy tiles and the weathered stone of the very old sculpture on the concrete plinth.*

Right: *A beautiful display of bark baskets in different shapes. You can clearly see the slatted base and how the separate branches are bound together with raffia. The soft pink colors of the flowers contrast with the dark brown of the rough bark.*

Wooden strawberries in a wooden basket

The "basket" on the right is deceptive; it is in fact an extremely beautiful dummy board painted with red strawberries. It is made of chipboard and is ideal for brightening up a gloomy corner. Dummy boards originated in America and England in the eighteenth century. In those days, they depicted dolls, small adults, and children. They were used to fill a space, to make a room look lived-in, and were meant to be looked at. When the owner of the house was absent, they were put in the window to suggest that the house was occupied. Flower scenes were popular in Victorian times; in summer, a panel might be placed in an empty fireplace, which is presumably why they were called summer screens. Today, dummy boards are popular once more. They are not only used in fireplaces, but also in windows, to hide an unattractive feature, or just as an interesting focal point. They are often miniature works of art. The patterns are not limited to flower baskets; bears, geese, ducks, and swans are popular subjects and many amateurs test their skill, making their own dummies out of pieces of hardboard.

Left and above: Dummy boards of blue hydrangeas and orange-red strawberries, painted by an Italian artist.

Baskets made from a variety of other woods

Not all baskets are made from willow or wood. They can be made from many materials and that is just what has happened through the ages. People have made baskets from whatever was handy, be it rush, as mentioned in the Bible, rags, or grass. The American settlers made baskets from old rolled-up papers.

At the moment, it is fashionable to make baskets from as many different woods as possible, and these are produced in countries with a plentiful supply of raw materials. The baskets might be made from broom, lavender, olive wood, laurel, or even ferns. Their main characteristic is that the material is clearly visible: the rough green of the broom, the prickly leaves of the olive tree, the fragrance of dried lavender flowers, the dried fan-shapes of the ferns, and the thick edges of rolled rush. All these baskets derive their particular charm from the obvious use of natural materials. The box baskets photographed on the left look as though they have been woven by someone who could not wait to start work and set to at the roadside as soon as the box was harvested. However, this is not the case. These beautiful baskets were first dyed to reinforce their natural color, and they remain pleasantly green even if they are not watered. If they were not treated in this way the baskets would soon dry out and turn brown, and the leaves would begin to drop. They would first become fall baskets and then look rather bare in winter.

Baskets are quite often made from a combination of willow and wood, particularly these days when functional and aesthetic values are equally important and people want baskets in many shapes and sizes. On the following pages we feature baskets made from a variety of woods, each one suited to the room it is displayed in.

Left: An array of box baskets piled up and ready for dispatch. They look a bit messy, but that is part of their charm.

Left: A mixture of ferns arranged in a shapely, dark brown basket. The textures complement each other well.

For example, the broad green broom edging around the basket on the inlaid Empire cupboard is important, as it rather dictates the color of the flowers that can be used in it; in fact, a broom basket like this would not suit every room. This basket is filled with several varieties of fern that match the broom beautifully, and lilies, grapes, red onions, *Euphorbia* leaves, and gray *Artemisia* are arranged among the ferns. The onions and grapes make a stylish contrast to the lilies.

Together, gray olive wood and brown willow make a strong pot hider in the classic 1920s gentleman's room. Red zinnias, red dahlias, ivy, and hosta leaves are interspersed with French beans in a red and green display. This elegant arrangement complements the portrait between the hunting trophies and the reddish-brown Victorian mahogany furniture.

In contrast to these formal rooms, the "edible" display on the right looks absolutely right against the Delft-blue tiles on a kitchen wall. A handmade jello mold hangs above the basket. The rolls in the basket are purely

Above left: *This round basket is a combination of willow and green broom.*

Left: *Willow and olive wood are combined in this attractively colored basket.*

Right: *A Spanish hanging basket made of broom, with a decorative arrangement of rolls. The natural green of the basket goes well with the "ingredients" of this unusual kitchen display.*

decorative. They are made from dough that contains a great deal of salt but no yeast. It will keep for years, especially if it is first varnished. The basket is filled with clay instead of flower foam, and the green foliage, corn, and rolls are fixed in the clay. The rolls are first fastened onto wire. Once the clay has dried, the arrangement is firmly anchored and looks good enough to eat!

The large, tulip-shaped baskets from Portugal featured opposite are woven out of dark willow. The small, loose bundles of willow twigs that form a carpet in the picture are nowadays sold in bundles. With a little imagination you can come up with ideas on how to use these bunches, from making a broom to hanging them on the Christmas tree with red ribbons.

In the background, birch twigs have been bound together to make a fence that can be used inside or outdoors. Used as a fence between two gardens, the twigs will shoot and make a natural green divider. Alternatively, you can use it as a windbreak on a patio or terrace, where the dark-colored screen will provide welcome natural shade.

Left: The distinctive tulip shape of these Portuguese baskets makes them ideal for plant and flower arrangements.

Baskets as containers — attractive and strong

Baskets have performed an important function in storage and transport. Different countries produce baskets made from whatever material is available. For example, in the Netherlands, weavers only use willow, whereas in France and Italy they favor chestnut as well as willow. Wide strips of chestnut make very characteristic baskets. Chairs are made from chestnut offcuts and are often erroneously called reed chairs. They are very popular because their structure and high round shapes are ideally suited to conservatories and gardens. In Spain, baskets are made from broom and olive wood, while rattan and bamboo are favored in the Far East, and strong grass and bulrushes are used to make baskets in Africa.

Baskets have always been designed for specific functions and were custom-made for each trade, so that the baker, butcher, gardener, farmer, grocer, and fisherman each had their own style.

Left: Bakers display their bread in baskets designed to hold loaves of many shapes and sizes.

Special baskets were also made for indoor use; we have all seen shopping baskets and dog baskets. These were all made from strong willow by expert basket makers until World War II. Then many things changed; we started using much cheaper, plastic packing materials or boxes and crates. Now we pack hardly anything in baskets, but the distinctive basket shapes are still preserved.

In the 1970s there was a revival of the basket and now in the 1990s they are fashionable again and used more and more around the house. Young mothers lay their babies in reed baskets, and dogs sleep in baskets specially made for them. Baskets can be decorative or functional, and their warmth and beauty have a universal appeal. They are also environmentally friendly – an increasingly important consideration these days. There is a particular demand today for old industrial baskets, but now we use them for

Left: Baskets on the back or front of bicycles save us using plastic bags for small purchases.

Above: The rectangular bakery baskets with shallow sides are custom-made for bakers. They fit exactly into a display window or on the counter, and years ago, they went on the baker's cart. In some countries, bread is still displayed in these baskets in bakers' shops. The two baskets with lids, the high round basket, and the square, flat basket are all laundry baskets. Wicker baskets are becoming more popular in the home.

Left: This French, open-weave laundry basket is being used to store linen.

other purposes, such as garden garbage, logs, or magazines. This is part of the appeal of these baskets; they are a nostalgic reminder of bygone years, and the people who buy them are attracted by their history and are pleased to find a suitable purpose for them in their homes today. Take the French open-weave laundry basket on page 75, for example; as well as laundry, you can use it to store and transport earthenware plant pots. It is solidly made and yet, being open-weave, it lets in air.

The basket on the right is made from center cane, a by-product of rattan, which was very popular in the 1950s. Center cane was used a great deal by amateur weavers, and the bleached version was especially popular. It was often used in a serving tray that has a lacquered three-ply board base and a rim of woven center cane.

Right: This old potato basket is a favorite family heirloom— a reminder of happy childhood days. And yet it still has a practical application today. It can take its place in a modern kitchen, where it is just as useful now for storing vegetables as it was before.

Storage baskets

Open-weave, stripped willow baskets are ideal for storing a variety of household items. You can see right away what is in the basket and whether it is running out. Baskets are also good for storing vegetables because their open-weave construction allows air to circulate around them, which keeps the produce fresh. At the bottom of the cupboard (shown top right) is an attractive wooden oyster crate. Originally, these crates were intended as packing cases for fresh oysters and were thrown away after use. However, if you clean them thoroughly, they are good for storing vegetables and fruit. This one has carrots in it, but you could also use it for onions – the smell of onions and fish together will do no harm. You could try scattering some ground coffee in the crate; the smell of the coffee will overpower the smell of the fish. Crates like this are also a cheap and attractive way of displaying plants.

Left: Strong bulb baskets, complete with their packing number, are popular today.

Top right: It is very satisfying to clean out and straighten up your cabinets and see everything neatly arranged in suitable baskets.

Bottom right: By tradition, the tall rag basket was made of unstripped willow, but this one is woven with strong lacquered rattan. As well as dust cloths, you can keep other cleaning materials in the baskets and carry them around the house.

Whether they are houseproud or not, Dutch housewives are very familiar with rag baskets and you will find one in every Dutch home. Modern manufacturers have tried to introduce metal boxes or ingenious plastic household kits to replace them, but without success. The baskets are mostly filled with an assortment of old rags, brushes, cans of wax, and even shoe polish.

Grape pickers traditionally used a basket or a wooden harvesting trough with a flat side so that it could be carried comfortably on the back. A small handle was connected to the flat side. Under the basket are wooden offcuts to improve the balance of the basket when it is full and to protect the base. When they were in regular use, the baskets were often left on wet clay or damp cellar floors.

It would be a waste to use such a practical and attractive basket just for picking grapes. As it has a flat side it makes an excellent container for a flower arrangement intended to stand against a wall or window. All the flowers face outwards and do not become trapped against the wall behind them.

Top left: *The basket on the white garden bench is filled with dark blue grapes harvested from the green branches that climb above and around the bench. Behind the bench is a bottle basket filled with the final product of the harvest.*

Bottom left: *Dahlias, grapes, pumpkins, ivies, and oak leaves in a stunning fall display.*

Left: *Giving full rein to your imagination can have unusual results. Here, an unsightly, green plastic mailbox is concealed in a custom-made basket. It is possible to have your own baskets made in all shapes and sizes by expert weavers. Sometimes the design proves to have a broader appeal, is then produced in greater quantities, and becomes more widely available.*

Left: *Yet another good idea for using tall storage baskets around the garden: convert them into two flower pillars next to a bench. We have fitted baskets of golden-yellow African marigolds inside the rim of the larger baskets. It is impossible to fill the whole basket with soil, as it would become too heavy to move, so first we placed a few stones at the bottom of the larger baskets to make them more stable. Later we decided to move the baskets to the entrance of the house. They are much too beautiful to stay in one place and it is exciting to experiment with them.*

All about wreaths, garlands, and other designs

Willow, rattan, and vine branches can be used to make all sorts of practical tools, as well as baskets and decorative objects for the home. All manner of things can be produced from basket material, and it is clear that in the past it was widely used to make everything from fences and roofs to lobster pots and muzzles for animals, dressmakers' dummies, and hoops for skirts and dresses. For generations, rugs were cleaned with a carpet beater made of woven rattan. Every household had one and every hall closet had a hook on which to hang it. However, carpet beaters are not much used these days, although they are still produced and used for decorative purposes.

Often, the warmth of the material is more important than its practicality, as people feel the need to surround themselves with natural things. These might take the form of exotic wooden shapes from the Philippines to the

Left: A range of everyday objects made from basketware. Shops specializing in these goods are a source of inspiration.

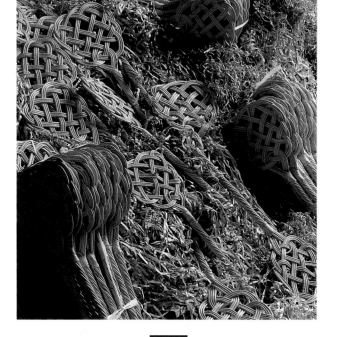

endearing little lambs standing in front of bundles of Dutch willow featured on page 84, also from the Philippines. They have been woven from twigs of vine and make a decorative feature both outside and indoors. When they are put in the garden or on a balcony or terrace, they become part of the green surroundings. Moss and weeds will start to grow on them, and a little slug may make its home inside them. Eventually, these little lambs will have their own life in your garden. Indoors, they are just as attractive and look at home wherever you put them, whether it is in front of antique oak furniture or in an ultra-modern room setting.

The same thing applies to the birdcage, which was also made in the Philippines. The symmetrical arrangement of branches is very pleasing to the eye, but this birdcage is only intended for decoration on a wall or in a corner of the house. Do not try to

Left: Cane carpet beaters were once considered an essential household item. Now they are valued more for decoration.

keep birds in it. However, you could put it outside in winter as a birdhouse. It looks attractive in the garden and is a useful sanctuary for wild birds when they are having a rough time in winter.

Wreaths

These days, wreaths are almost commonplace in our homes and feature not only at Christmastime, but also throughout the year. Wreaths made of olive wood are prickly and tough. They look beautiful hanging on the front door, where they will eventually weather and become an indeterminate shade of gray-green. Some olive wood garlands have icicle shapes on either side, just where you hang the garland up on nails, and it is very tempting to arrange some large gray-green or burnished red, earthy-colored paper ribbons directly above the icicles. Most of these very pretty garlands, and the olive wood and broom wreaths, come from Spain.

Above left: These little lambs make an eye-catching display wherever they are.

Left: You could decorate this birdcage with dried flowers, gourds, nuts or a pomander.

Right: Wreaths can be woven in a variety of materials. These are made from broom and olive wood. The chalky white ones are quite stiff; you can decorate them with paper ribbons.

Above: Wreaths made of broom, olive, and vine wood are stacked alongside baskets full of apples.

Right: Fragrant wooden trees fill the room with a fresh country scent.

The small trees made of olive wood, thyme, and laurel on the right are also made in Spain. Besides being very decorative, they also produce a lovely aromatic perfume, so that the room is soon filled with a pervasive fragrance. The stems are old and knotted, and the thyme, olive, or laurel leaves are ingeniously connected to the stems so that they resemble bonsai trees. The little trees are placed in baskets made of the same wood. Although these trees smell wonderful, you cannot use them for culinary purposes. For cooking, you must buy herbs in special jars or bags, or grow your own in the garden.

A hollow, woven willow ball has many uses. At Christmas, you can decorate it with little bows, dried flowers, colored balls, a little foliage, or with fir cones, so that it looks like a wooden Christmas tree. Another idea is to decorate it with a large ribbon, some holly, and little baubles. During the rest of the year you could fill it with ivy plants that soon grow over the edge of the ball. If you hang it in the garden, moss and plants will soon grow on it. You can try hanging the ball upside down on a wall, so that it becomes a large hanging basket where you can store all kinds of things, including fruit and vegetables in the kitchen. It also makes a cheerful arrangement for the living room, a place to store brushes in the workshop or shed, or a place to keep tennis or

golf balls. Let your imagination loose and do not be afraid to experiment with these versatile willow shapes.

Thick lavender wreaths suspended on a lavender-blue silk ribbon smell wonderful in a bathroom or in the bedroom. Fat bundles of rush bound together make thick, lush wreaths, and untidy vine branches make untidy, typically French wreaths. And, of course, we have all seen willow wreaths, both dark ones and light-colored, stripped wreaths. You might think that these would all be produced in their native countries, but in fact they are manufactured by the thousands in China.

Above: *This open-weave wreath, woven around a wooden base, is another variation. Both round and oval shapes are available. You can make a floral wreath by putting a ring of flower foam around the edge and arranging the blooms in the foam, or you could put in night lights or little candles. Try hanging the wreaths on a wall or, as here, placing them on a table on a bed of virginia creeper* (Parthenocissus quinquefolia). *Roses, broom, and lemon-scented geranium* (Pelargonium graveolens) *are tucked between the little glasses holding the night lights.*

Rattan furniture

Rattan furniture has been manufactured and used throughout the ages. It was particularly popular during the Victorian period when houses were filled with it and rattan found its way into every room, into the hall, and into conservatories and gardens. It was also considered very stylish to have an oriental room, completely furnished with rattan furniture, bamboo wallpaper, and pedestals, all evoking a tropical atmosphere.

What was the secret of rattan? Why was it so popular? Well, rattan is a natural product, the furniture is handmade and very comfortable. Furthermore, it is both exotic and rustic, old and, at the same time, up-to-date. As a matter of fact, all these factors are still relevant and account for the revival in the popularity of rattan furniture today. We have the same requirements as the Victorians, and rattan, sumptuous silky fabrics, and terracotta are all very fashionable again. After a period of cold, white interior decor, we now look for more warmth in our furnishings, and rattan fulfills this desire for natural materials.

The furniture is made in the Far East, where manufacturing costs are much lower than in the West. Rattan is generally affordable and we now see more and more rattan furniture decorating conservatories, gardens, and patios, as well as rooms indoors.

Above: Rattan is a natural choice for garden furniture, being both comfortable and practical. Magazines and books on interior design often feature room settings like this to show how to use rattan around the home.

Above: *Rattan chairs are available in a vast range of styles, shapes, and sizes.*

Right: *This splendid woven willow parasol is a superb combination of the beautiful, the natural, and the functional. It measures 10' (3 m) in diameter and gives the garden an exotic air. For the people sitting underneath this parasol, it is cool and pleasant, and the* *natural oasis of filtered light is also ideal for shade-loving plants. The metal shaft supporting the parasol is buried in a concrete block, which is disguised with baskets full of plants, including* Ampelopsis brevipedunculata *'Variegata' and gray* Santolina. *The wooden chair is made in the style of the recliners used on the decks of cruise ships during* *the 1920s. Being made of teak, the chair can remain outside all year. In fact, it becomes more attractive with age – as the color fades, it seems to acquire a genuine old patina.*

Fall tints — dried flowers in wicker

Dried summer flowers acquire a fall character that seems a perfect match for the natural brown of wicker and wooden baskets. The wooden stems with their crispy petals seem to be growing naturally out of the variously shaped willow, broom, or olive wood containers. The photograph on the left shows how the bright colors of the dried flower arrangement are reflected in the brocades and silks that surround it.

There are various methods of drying flowers and foliage. We used an old-fashioned method to dry the ferns and raspberry leaves featured in the arrangement on page 96. Why old-fashioned you may ask? Well, because it entails using rugs, which are not so common in these days of wall-to-wall carpets, linoleum, and tiled and timbered floors. To dry the ferns and leaves, first put a layer of paper on the floor and then carefully place the leaves on top. Cover

them with a second layer of papers, and finally cover the whole thing with rugs or carpets. After the leaves have been walked over for several weeks, they will be dry. This old way of drying leaves has proved very successful and is well worth trying.

Dried flower displays need not be confined to a domestic setting. Doctors and dentists have found that, like tropical fish tanks, flowers can have a beneficial effect on the sterile and sometimes frightening environment of a waiting room. One dentist installed a basket of peonies with a lavender-covered handle in her office. It hangs on the wall opposite the patient's chair, and the beautiful flowers provide a distraction and a lively topic of conversation in the treatment room. Patients forget their pain, and tension and fear are relieved. It seems that flowers have unexpected therapeutic qualities.

Left: Bouquets of dried flowers are extremely well-suited to this elegant 18th-century salon with its stylish furniture, sculptures, and valuable accessories.

Left: A basket made of broom with an elegant handle. Filled with invitations, it nestles in the fall sunshine amid a mass of beautiful dried blooms.

Above: The oblong basket standing in this impressive hallway is just 2" (5 cm) wide. Its very large handle has been covered with moss, and small bunches of raffia and lavender are fixed to the moss. The basket is filled with dried peonies, hydrangeas, lavender, Santolina, *and wild strawberry leaves (*Duchesnea indica*). The whole arrangement is surrounded by leaves blown in by the wind.

Right: If you are going to dry hydrangeas, it is a good idea to stand them upright in a large basket once they have been picked. This minimizes the risk of the flowers being damaged.

Drying lavender and peonies

To dry lavender, pick it just before it is in full flower and hang small bunches in a dry, dark, airy room. They will be dry and ready to use within one or two days. Do not dry them for too long, and do not leave them to dry on the plant, as they will fade and the flowers will soon drop.

To dry peonies, hang them up as soon as you have picked them – never put them in water first. If you do not have peonies in your garden, buy them when the flowers are open and hang them up right away.

Above: These peonies in shades of pink are gathered together in a large basket, waiting to be arranged into a colorful fall bouquet. Do not put them in water if they are to be dried.

Left: *This charming basket made of broom is filled with golden-yellow, gray, and white flowers, and foliage, and stands on an étagère, or ornamental stand, made from 18th-century roofing material. A semicircular basket is ideal in a position against a wall or, as here, a mirror. A mirror is particularly effective, as it reflects the flowers and transforms the semicircular bouquet into a round one.*

Right: *Although they are dried, the plants in this display, which include peonies, hydrangeas, rudbeckias, and ferns, still retain much of their original, dazzling color.*

Left: *These sunflowers were carefully dried upside down in some sand. The fallen petals were reattached to the stems with a glue gun.*

Above: *An arrangement of dried yellow* Helianthus *flowers graces a table amid pieces of Fortuny silk and two stone hands, lovingly clasped together.*

Right: An open-weave, aluminum basket on a chair with a woven back and seat. The basket is lined with dried moss and filled mostly with paper. A layer of flower foam is placed on top of the paper and the flowers are then arranged in this.

Left: *A red-painted basket from Thailand standing on a green metal table. Matching braid has been threaded through the open weave at the top of the basket, and the flowers include hydrangeas, dried peonies, and specially treated red beech leaves. The best way to dry hydrangeas is to hang them in bunches in a dark, airy room. This works very well if the hydrangeas were picked during dry weather and their flowers are already dry and crispy. However, if you prefer brightly colored flowers, pick them at the height of their flowering period and dry them in sand. Before you arrange them, support small bunches of the flowers with wire.*

Left: *Long ivy branches entwine themselves around an open-weave basket containing a subtly colored dried flower arrangement.*

Right: *An old, open-weave wire basket has been sprayed white and now holds a metal bowl with a varied display of flowers. They have all been dried in sand, hence their bright colors. The two pumpkins next to them on the round table add to the fall atmosphere and are a delightful decorative feature in their own right.*

Whenever you cut a pumpkin in half, take a good look inside, because you often find a seed that has started to sprout. These beautiful little masterpieces can be used to decorate the kitchen or plant table.

Festive baskets for Easter and Christmas

In early spring, when the sun beckons us outside, it is tempting to eat outdoors and to lay the table in the garden, perhaps for an Easter meal. In the photograph on the left, vases on the table full of the first lilies-of-the-valley (*Convallaria majalis*) accompany a festive strawberry basket of white daisies (*Chrysanthemum*), their yellow centers matching the bee-yellow of the begonias. *Anthriscus sylvestris,* a European wildflower, tumbles over the edge of the basket and an extravagant white ribbon accentuates the festive nature of the setting. The small candlesticks were chosen because their green shades, decorated with hand-painted primroses, match the yellow spring flowers so well. Garden ornaments also include beautiful fiberglass troughs, copies of old papier-mâché jardinières. The original jardinières look beautiful, but are not usually waterproof. However, the modern

Left: Strawberry baskets hang on the willow trees above an inviting brunch table. They are filled with begonias, Anthriscus sylvestris, *dead nettle, and ivy.*

and very attractive copies are waterproof and it is quite safe to arrange plants and bouquets in them, and then place them on valuable furniture without any danger that they might leave marks. They are quite easy to obtain and less expensive than the rare antique originals.

A large ball of flower foam forms the basis of the flowering "trees" in baskets pictured below, and bright orange tulips highlight the whole arrangement. You could use any free-flowering wildflowers, such as wild, or white, chervil (*Cryptotaenia*) or Queen Anne's Lace (*Daucus carota* var. *carota*), to make up a similar display. Do not wait too long before picking the plants, because once they have grown tall, people mow them down. Put them in pots and tubs in the garden, or on patios, where everyone can enjoy them. Wild chervil keeps well outside, but indoors the flowers soon drop, making a white carpet on the ground.

Left: Wild flowers have been used to create this elegant "tree" in a basket. The delicate white flowers bring a breath of the countryside into the garden.

Above: The Easter theme is reflected everywhere, even on the shed wall and in the box leaf bow with a chick made of dough in the middle. You can also see it in the bread wreath decorated with herbs and another chick. On the semicircular table, more chicks and cockerels made of bread sit invitingly among the mouth-watering rolls arranged in two baskets made of broom.

Above: *The centerpiece of this beautiful Easter display, proudly set on a plinth in the middle of the garden, is a wooden hen brooding her eggs on the nest. A garland of rolls and variously colored marbled eggs surrounds the rough wicker* basket. *A hen's nest with straw on top is a good theme for a basket display and looks very attractive in the spring garden. The hen can remain in place long after the bread and eggs have been plundered by your visitors. For a more* permanent feature, you could make a garland of box twigs and herbs. The red flowers of a spring-flowering azalea (Rhododendron schlippenbachii) *make a fitting backdrop for this eye-catching, seasonal nest.*

Baskets for Christmas

In the dark days before Christmas, people appreciate extra warmth and like to feel snug, so we decorate our homes with plenty of flowers, fruit, and foliage. You could say that we bring nature indoors and adorn her with ribbons and shiny decorations. When the days are short and it is cold and damp outside, we can bring an oasis of fragrant foliage, color, and warmth inside.

A warm welcome awaits visitors to the house featured on the right in the form of a bright arrangement of yellow, white, and green in a semicircular hanging basket on the front door. Daffodils, *Euphorbia* leaves, and variegated ivy are arranged in damp flower foam, with sticks of cinnamon tied in a blue jute ribbon. As long as the temperature remains above freezing, even if it is cold and damp, the arrangement will keep for weeks. If it turns frosty, however, you must bring it inside. The garland of fir cones with the same blue ribbon can remain outside all winter. It makes a welcome change to have something quite different from the traditional Christmas wreath on the door.

Inside, the fire is lit (right) and baskets hold the materials to keep it going, such as logs, firewood, and fir cones. Another basket is filled with sweet chestnuts ready for roasting, and cinnamon sticks supply an aromatic

Above: Bring spring color to the front door with a cheerful hanging basket.

Right: Baskets grouped around the hearth add their own golden glow to the fire.

fragrance. The cinnamon sticks are stored in a basket intended for harvesting cherries. It is tall but not very large and has a long handle so that the cinnamon sticks can stand upright. On the hearth is a so-called potato basket with an open-weave base. The potatoes are harvested and shaken in the basket to get rid of the soil.

A Danish Christmas tree

The pine tree on this page, a spruce (*Picea glauca*), has a beautiful shape and will not drop its needles. It looks most attractive with its silver and white glass decorations, and it is crowned by an angel that has been in the family for years. She was made in France out of papier-mâché, but her head and hands are made of wax. Every year, she is carefully taken out of tissue paper and placed on top of the tree. The presents underneath the tree are displayed in colored aluminum baskets. These have become very popular once again. We have seen how effective they look when filled with flowers and foliage (see page 100), but here they have been put to quite different use.

The Christmas tree is illuminated with a mass of lights, reflected like a fairytale in the large golden mirror on the opposite wall.

Left: *The delicate tracery of these aluminum baskets reveals the presents inside.*

Opposite the Christmas tree, a nativity scene is set out on a carpet of dried rose petals. The dough figures were made by children many years ago and are brought out of their box every year. The white, wooden angels come from Germany. Green-and-white hydrangeas (*Hydrangea macrophylla* 'Mme. Emily Mouiller') and variegated ivy fill the beribboned, dark wicker basket and enhance the Christmas scene depicted around them.

Above: Christmas is a time for tradition and it is fun to bring out decorations that have become a part of family history. They retain their freshness from year to year.

The green color of broom evokes the Christmas atmosphere particularly well and explains why so many broom decorations are available at this time of year, from bells to wreaths and animal shapes. A small broom Christmas tree is ideal for people who are

short of space or, as shown above, want to decorate an area under the stairs. This rooted spruce (*Picea glauca* 'Conica') is planted in a basket and decorated with small pieces of dried flowers. If there is plenty of space, you could try arranging three small trees in a row instead of one large one, or stand them outside the door. The round tree on the table is from Spain and is made of broom needles glued onto a branch of broom that forms the

tree stem. The whole thing is then placed in a broom basket. Behind the table decorations is an unusual card holder in the shape of a Christmas tree made of three-ply board. It is suspended from a grass garland decorated with ribbon. After Christmas you can hang up the garland without the tree. American silk ribbon is wound around the banisters. The ribbon has thin wire at each edge that allows you to twist it into any shape.

Far left: A selection of attractive Christmas decorations that you can adapt to suit your home.

Left: As a change from the usual pine and fir, there are other materials that evoke a Christmas atmosphere. Here, for example, a garland made of ivy is arranged on the mantelpiece above the fireplace, and a straw teddy bear with a tartan ribbon around his neck carries a basket decorated with the same ribbon. The bear has been modeled with straw onto little sticks, and the straw is held in place with wire. The bear's straw body smells lovely and you can leave him to grow very old. He is sitting next to a small rooted fir tree in a basket, similar to the one on page 112. This tree is decorated with cooking pears and bunches of cinnamon sticks tied with the same ribbon as you see around the bear's neck. The shiny red apples are stacked in a strong Dutch handcrafted basket.

Above: For a truly stunning outdoor display, two rooted conifers have been planted in enormous packing baskets. They are decorated with seasonal orange mandarins, red pomegranates, green lemons, green cooking pears, bright red apples, and open, red-and-green miniature cabbages, interspersed with dried hydrangeas. Large jute ribbons and trailing variegated ivies add the finishing touches to these very unusual and special Christmas trees.

Right: Back inside, delicate champagne-colored roses, milky-white lilies, tulips, and fragrant eucalyptus leaves are arranged in a square basket.

Left: The upright stems of white Christmas roses (Helleborus niger) are surrounded by delicate light-green ferns. The cool colors of the flowers and foliage are echoed in the matt-green, moiré silk ribbon around the basket. The basket is standing on a white-marbled, Empire-style table, while underneath the table, a replica of Aphrodite, the Greek goddess of love and beauty, gazes modestly at the ground.

Right: From a cool, green-and-white arrangement indoors to a warm, red display outside. Here, bright red poinsettias and variegated ivy are arranged in a wicker basket on a table by a welcoming fire.

More festive baskets for parties and a wedding

Decorations for parties are a regular part of any flower arranger's profession, and although it may sound an easy job, days of planning, working out ideas, and buying special items at auctions, precede the actual flower-arranging. The displays on these pages were commissioned for a dinner party in an old manor house. Two rooms were used: one for the older guests and one for the young ones. The tables in the young people's room were decorated with pale pink colors, while the older generation enjoyed a blue theme.

Baskets were used to hold all the displays, including the large one on the 19th-century mantelpiece on the left. The long, oval basket easily fits the space and is filled with white delphiniums, peonies, lilies, *Trachelium*, and ivy. A semicircular panel on the rectangular mirror behind it depicts a golden Venus, and the black marble mantelpiece is decorated with reliefs of Roman heads and young

cupids. Three-branched, brass candlesticks hang on either side of the mirror.

There is a striking contrast between the elegant place settings on the dining tables and the delicacy of the flowers on the one hand, and the the roughness of the baskets in which the flowers are arranged on the other. And yet the combination works very well, as is clear from the picture below. On the long tables in what was the billiard room and is to be the "blue" room for this occasion, large, dark brown wicker baskets are the containers chosen to show off the subtle shades of *Lathyrus*, roses, and ferns. The blue theme is accentuated by blue ribbons. On the round tables in the "pink" room shown on page 120, pale pink *Lathyrus*, *Alchemilla mollis*, and long branches of ivy are set among the candlesticks decorated with pink ribbons. Each table has a different color ribbon, which helps the guests to find their places as they enter the room.

Left: *A mirror makes an ideal backdrop for a semicircular arrangement like this, as it reflects the flowers from behind.*

Left: *Building a flower display around one color can be very effective. You can continue the theme with ribbons and candles.*

A wedding, flowers, and baskets

Nothing is more inspiring than creating floral decorations for a wedding. The beautiful arrangement on the windowsill on the right combines peonies, delphiniums, *Alchemilla*, *Rosa* 'Veronica', and *Rosa* 'Jacaranda'. The wedding cake will eventually be placed on the heart-shaped garland on the table. Sheaves of wheat tied with pink ribbon stand on either side of the window, and two stylized, wooden water birds complete this charming picture.

Above left: The shades of the summer bouquet on the mantelpiece are picked up by the decorations on the tables.

Below left: A heart-shaped arrangement hangs on the bride and groom's front door.

Right: What could be more romantic than this pastel-colored still life? The heart-shaped centerpiece on the table includes Lathyrus *and* Alchemilla mollis, *which are also used in the garland on the house door.*

Left: *The first step is to buy the flowers. Then they are sorted by color and plunged into buckets of water. The buckets then go into baskets to await the attentions of the flower arranger. These sturdy baskets are filled with pink ranunculus, pink and champagne-colored roses, blue delphiniums, cream foxgloves, pink and white lilies, and orange-yellow fritillarias, with their delightful nodding heads.*

Above right: *All the flowers in the church are arranged in baskets. The dark brown of the wicker matches the dark oak furnishings of the church quite beautifully and sets off the pale shades of the flowers. Delphiniums, roses, foxgloves, along with* Campanula medium *'Calycanthema'*, Viburnum opulus *'Roseum' (the Guelder rose), cream stocks (Matthiola), and white lilies all help to soften the rigid simplicity of the interior of the church. Light from the candles in the brass chandeliers shines down on the flowers. The result is cheerful but restrained, totally in keeping with the church surroundings.*

Below right: *Outside the little church, two pretty hydrangea trees in large wicker apple baskets await the bride and groom. Geraniums of the same color as the hydrangeas (Pelargonium 'Black Knight') are planted at the base of the hydrangea tree, and ribbons and bows wave a warm welcome.*

Baskets in history — still in use today

Baskets have always been regarded as an irreplaceable packing medium for trade and export. They were used in the marketplace, in agricultural life, and in the household. Potatoes, fruit, peat, bulbs, cheese, candles, laundry, bread, and vegetables – all have played a vital part in world economy, and all have had baskets made for them, which in turn became as essential as the goods contained in them.

We know that in ancient Egypt, people made baskets, rugs, bags, nets, handles for cooking pots, brooms, brushes, and sandals out of vegetable materials. The Egyptians employed several weaving techniques, depending on the material and the purpose for which the product was intended. Mats made of palm leaves and used for the burial of the dead have been found in Egyptian tombs. These old mats date from about 4500 B.C. Baskets are

Left: Placing chickens in a purpose-made basket seems a humane method of transporting them. They can see out and have access to plenty of fresh air.

mentioned in the Bible, among them the baskets that the spies brought back from the Promised Land.

In England, a Basket Makers Company, or Crafts Guild, was established in London in 1569. However, it is certain that basket makers were practicing their trade long before this, as they were included in the Crafts List of the Brewers Company, a document dating back to 1422. In the Netherlands, a Basket Makers Guild was founded in 1579 and the Jacobi Church in Utrecht became the Guild's own church.

The Wicker and Basket Foundation in the Netherlands owns a collection of old, traditional baskets. Among other things, the Foundation aims to acquire materials of historical value and to originate and support research and studies within this field. The Foundation wishes to bring wicker and baskets

Left: These baskets for fish are equipped with lids and are ideal for storing your catch while you are out on a fishing trip, and then carrying it safely home.

Above: A memorial plaque belonging to the Utrecht Basket Makers Guild in the Jacobi Church in Utrecht. They were given their own guild vault in 1639 and the plaque is inscribed with three Biblical stories that each mention baskets.

to the attention of as many people as possible. Nowadays, many people regard old baskets as collectors' items. They love them for their toughness and decorative appeal and appreciate the many techniques that went into their manufacture. Old baskets exude a nostalgic atmosphere – after all, history is reflected in their color and patina, in their worn-out basketwork, and misshapen forms. When we look at them, we wonder what sort of stories they could tell us!

Whether we examine a farmer's old shopping basket, a basket that once held vintage champagne, baskets for chicken or fish, rusty wire baskets for eggs, or antique silver bread baskets on richly laid tables, we find something special in each one. They have been used for years and have acquired their own history.

Above: *This old oblong basket was made specially to fit on the windowsill and has been in the family for generations. They continue to display their plants in this treasured heirloom.*

Above: *The silver wire basket in the library is an old bread basket. These were often used in hotels, which also had special baskets for wine bottles and biscuits. In this staid and rather dignified room, the bread basket is arranged with dark red peonies, red valerian,* *and green pea pods, still attached to their stems. They add a frivolous note to a rather solemn bouquet. A glass bowl has been put inside the silver wire basket to protect it, and the flowers are arranged in the glass bowl. You could use all kinds of baskets in this way.*

Right: *This antique brass basket is another family heirloom. It is standing on a round mirror to reflect its golden shine and is filled with an arrangement of fall flowers: red roses, clusters of attractive snowberries (Symphoricarpos albus), red Achillea, pink Calla,* *masterwort (Astrantia major), thistle, and ivies. The table has been laid in "hunting style." The china and crystal have gold rims to match the brass basket. Beside the dinner plates, potatoes cooked in their skins and decorated with a lily await the pheasant.*

Right: An antique silver basket makes a dazzling container for a table decoration. Remember to water the flowers regularly to keep them fresh.

Right: White lilies are shown off to perfection in this beautifully shaped, silver bread basket.

Practical ways of using baskets

The preceding chapters have featured a wide range of baskets, both with and without flowers and plants. On the following pages you will find practical advice on how to use baskets, how to line them, and what sort of material works best. We will discuss the ways in which the baskets can be used: there are baskets for plants and shrubs for the garden and the house; baskets used as a vase for cut fresh flowers; baskets for displays of fresh and dried flowers; and wire baskets for plants and dried flower arrangements.

Baskets for outdoor plants

If you are going to keep baskets in the garden or on the balcony, put them on planks about ⅜"–¾" (1–2 cm) thick. This will allow excess water to drain through the basket and also ensures that the basket is not left standing on damp soil or on a wet floor. The base should remain dry and will not decay. Before planting anything inside it, first line the basket with plastic. In small baskets, you could use old plastic shopping bags, provided they are gray, brown, or black. Gray or black trash bags are very useful in large baskets, and if a basket is very large, you can line it with a sheet of polythene. It is important to use a naturally colored liner as it will always be visible through the basket. Fit the plastic loosely inside the basket or attach it to the rim with large sewing stitches, as illustrated in the diagram below. Make sure that the thread you use is suitably thick and the appropriate color for both basket and liner. Make a few holes in the base of the plastic liner so that water can drain away.

As most baskets are very light, they are sometimes blown over when the weather is windy. It is a good idea, therefore, to take the precaution of weighting them down, either by putting some heavy stones in the base of the basket on top of the liner, or by adding a layer of gravel or clay granules.

Put a layer of sphagnum moss over the stones or gravel and then stand the plant roots on the moss. Fill the basket with more moss

and press it down firmly. Damp sphagnum moss is a very good growing medium for planted baskets. It is lighter than soil and retains water longer. It does not rot and contains many plant nutrients. In the past, you could only buy sphagnum moss at Christmastime, but nowadays it is available all year round from florists and garden centers. If you prefer not to use sphagnum moss, choose a good-quality potting mixture..

You can also keep indoor plants in baskets. Prepare the baskets in exactly the same way as described for outdoor plants with one important exception. Although drainage is important, do not make holes in the plastic lining of indoor baskets, because water may seep through and damage the furniture. To ensure that plants remain healthy, take care not to overwater them. You need not stand indoor baskets on planks.

Planting up a basket

Ivy is a useful filler for baskets and can remain in the container even when you replace other plants. It will continue to grow for many years, becoming greener and bushier, and eventually it forms a permanent green covering around the outside of the basket. Buy an ivy with long trailing stems, remove it from its pot and divide it into several individual plants. Plant the trailing stems into the sphagnum moss, one next to the other around the rim of the basket. Press the moss down firmly. Entwine the stems around each other and fix them to the rim of the basket with small lengths of florists' wire. Plant a seasonal flowering plant in the center of the basket – a primrose, for example – and when it finishes flowering, replace it with, say, an impatiens.

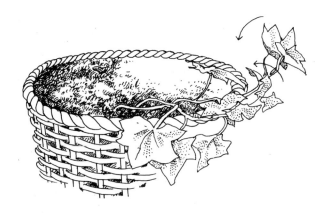

Large baskets with fresh flowers

Baskets make very suitable substitutes for flower vases, as the material and color of rough wicker baskets combine well with flowers and leaves. The colors of the blooms are heightened when contrasted with the dark brown wicker.

Start by putting a bucket – preferably a brown one – in a large basket and weight it with a stone. It is not easy to arrange flowers in a bucket, as they do not stay in the desired position and tend to slide away. To solve this problem, put a ball of chicken wire in the bucket and arrange the flowers individually in the wire. Choose 2" (5 cm) wire mesh, as it is impossible to fix flower stems into ⅜" (1 cm) mesh. Spread the chicken wire inside the bucket as evenly as possible. If the ball is too small, the arrangement will move and fall out of the bucket; if it is too large or dense, it will be impossible to push the stems through the holes. Fix the wire mesh to the side of the bucket with three pieces of waterproof tape, and then fill the bucket with water.

Small baskets of flowers

To make an arrangement in a small basket, you could use a plastic bowl or a glass jar as the inner container and weight it down with pebbles or marbles. Then put chicken wire into the bowl to hold the flower arrangement.

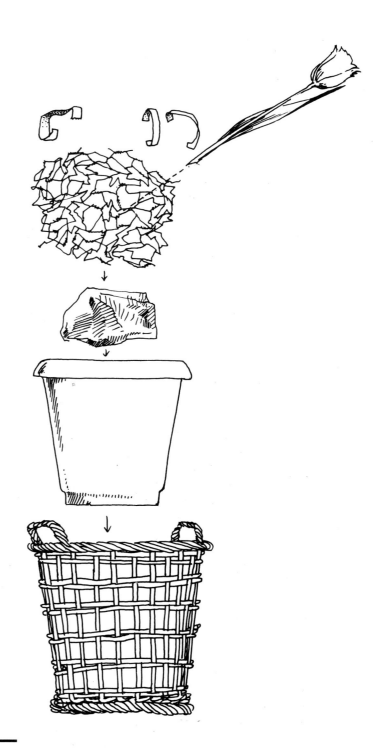

Baskets with an arrangement of fresh flowers in flower foam

You can use all kinds of plastic containers to line baskets, including ice cream tubs or plastic food containers, depending on the shape of the basket you want to fill. Once you have chosen the container, cut a piece of flower foam to the exact size of the inside of the bowl. It should sit ⅜" (1 cm) below the rim of the container. If the foam is too small, it will float and the arrangement may fall over. Ensure that the foam is firmly secured by covering it with chicken wire, taking the wire over the rim of the bowl, and attaching it with waterproof tape. Be sure to soak the flower foam thoroughly before putting it in the bowl.

Making a circular arrangement

In a round display, the flower stems are anchored into the flower foam at an angle around an imaginary central point (see the diagram top right). All the stems should point towards the center and should never cross each other above the rim of the basket.

The length of the stems determines the eventual size of the bouquet. Cut the stems diagonally and start by fixing all the foliage in circles round the center. This foliage forms the outline of the bouquet, and the flowers you add later on should not extend beyond this outline (see the diagram below right). Take

advantage of the natural twists in the stems and do not forget that each flower has a face.

Always arrange the flowers so that they face outwards. When the flowers are still in bud, it is easy to forget about the direction they are facing, so that when they open later on, you find that they are all pointing in different directions. A round bouquet should look attractive from all angles, so keep turning the arrangement as you work.

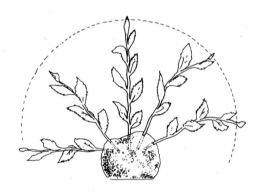

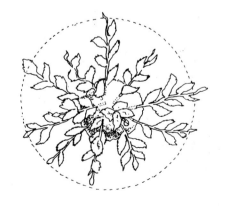

Baskets with dried flowers

To make a dried flower arrangement, start by lining a basket with plastic or choose one that already has a plastic lining. Put a piece of flower foam designed for dried flowers into the basket so that it sits about 2" (5 cm) above the rim of the container. Fix the foam to the rim with florists' wire or tape. If there are any gaps around the edge of the basket, fill them with old paper or dry sphagnum moss.

Next, cover the top of the flower foam with a layer of dry sphagnum moss. In this way, the base of the bouquet will look attractive and you will need fewer flowers to fill out the arrangement. Specialist shops offer a huge selection of dried flowers for arranging.

Making a bouquet with dried flowers

In the fall, you can arrange the flowers that you have picked and dried during the summer. First assemble all the leaves and flowers, and sort them by color and type.

Any flowers with weak stems or broken blooms can be supported with wire. Florists' wire is available in various thicknesses, from ¼" (6 mm) for delicate flowers to ⅜" (1 cm) for thicker-stemmed blooms. You can use wire for flowers that have been dried in sand and also tie up small bunches of flowers with wire.

There are many ways of using wire. You can wind it around a stem or, if a thin wooden skewer was used when drying the flower, remove the skewer and put some wire in the little hole. Make a small hook at one end of the wire and carefully pull the hook to the center of the flower. Fragile flowers with no stems can also be supported by putting a hook in the center of the flower (see diagram below). Wire is also essential for supporting the cones or nuts that sometimes feature in dried flower displays.

When you make a dried flower arrangement, you must start with a firm base of leaves. Make a low outline by, for example, pushing prepared beech leaves into some flower foam. Next, fix three twigs on top of the flower foam and, lower down, another five twigs between the upper rim and the first outline. Fill the space between the leaves with *Alchemilla mollis*, or lady's mantle, which is perfectly suitable as a filler in a dried bouquet. Its yellowish-green color functions as both leaf and flower. Now fix one twig at the top of the bouquet in the center, three more around it, and, a little lower down, five or seven twigs in the outline.

You now have a firm base of leaves and *Alchemilla*. You could use *Limonium*, or sea-lavender, instead of *Alchemilla*. Now insert each flower stem individually into the base. Arrange dark-colored and dense, round blooms lower down. Do not make the bouquet too dense; allow some of the flowers to protrude, particularly if you have some drooping, light-colored blossom. This will give the bouquet a delicate, ethereal feeling.

Take a good look at the bouquet when it is finished and, if there are any holes, fill them up with any remaining flowers.

Wire baskets with plants

Different wire baskets all have one thing in common: they are open and need some kind of liner. The liner will be visible because the mesh is often quite wide, so it is important to use a natural material, such as small pieces of sphagnum moss. Build up the moss against the sides of the basket and then put in a plastic liner. Fill the basket with damp sphagnum or potting mixture, and then it is ready for planting.

Wire baskets with dried flowers

If the basket is to be used for dried flowers, line it first with moss, but there is no need to add a plastic liner. Fill the basket three-quarters full of paper pellets and then put a piece of dry flower foam on top. Attach the flower foam to the rim of the basket with pieces of wreath wire. Cover the top of the flower foam with moss and then it is ready for the dried flowers. Fix the leaves and flowers into the flower foam through the moss.

Wire hanging baskets

The mesh in wire hanging baskets is much larger than in ordinary baskets, so the first stage is to line the basket with ⅜" (1 cm) chicken wire. Cover this with a layer of sphagnum or pieces of moss and then add a black plastic liner. Now the basket is ready to be filled with damp sphagnum moss for the plants. Always try to use sphagnum moss: it contains the food and water the plants would normally obtain from the soil. Plant as many plants as possible in the baskets; the aim is to achieve a delightful flowering ball that will continue to bloom for many months.

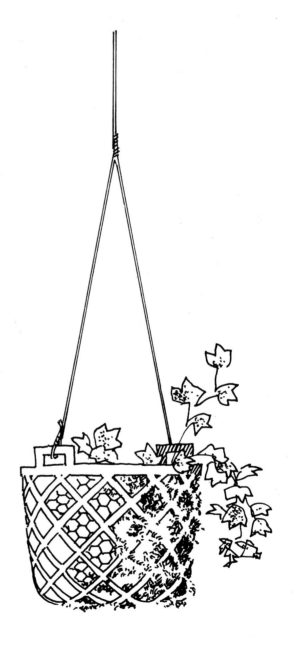

Finally and gratefully

In the course of preparing this book, we have seen a great many baskets from different countries, baskets made of different materials, and in all shapes and sizes. Each basket has told its own story; it was made by hand, whether by the old, rough hands of a Dutch basket maker or the graceful hands of a Philippino girl. All of them have made their baskets honestly, firmly, artistically and skillfully. And all the baskets have found an owner and a use. They were used in the past and they are still in use today.

We filled the baskets with magical, colorful arrangements of flowers, twigs, leaves, foliage, fruit, and vegetables, and then photographed the results to show them off to their best advantage.

Many people gave us their assistance, supplying their expertise, their materials, and their stories. It is unusual to write a book in isolation, and particularly during the creation of this book we have met many people like ourselves who love baskets, are interested in them, and make their living through them. We were allowed to borrow some exciting examples and to photograph them in beautiful locations, which showed our work at its very best. We wish to thank all the people who gave their time so willingly and generously during the course of our research.

ᕱ *Index* ᕱ